CATASTROPHILIA

ESSENTIAL POETS SERIES 320

Canada Council for the Arts
Conseil des Arts du Canada

ONTARIO ARTS COUNCIL
CONSEIL DES ARTS DE L'ONTARIO
an Ontario government agency
un organisme du gouvernement de l'Ont

Canada

Guernica Editions Inc. acknowledges the support of the Canada Council for the Arts and the Ontario Arts Council. The Ontario Arts Council is an agency of the Government of Ontario.

We acknowledge the financial support of the Government of Canada.

JULIE ROORDA

CATASTROPHILIA

TORONTO – BUFFALO – LANCASTER (U.K.)

2026

Copyright © 2026, Julie Roorda and Guernica Editions Inc.
All rights reserved. The use of any part of this publication, reproduced, transmitted in any form or by any means, electronic, mechanical, photocopying, recording or otherwise stored in a retrieval system, without the prior consent of the publisher is an infringement of the copyright law.
This material is protected by copyright law and may not be used for machine learning, AI training, or data mining without explicit written permission. This includes, but is not limited to, the use of text, images, and other content for the development of AI models.

Guernica founder: Antonio D'Alfonso

Michael Mirolla, editor
Cover and interior design: Errol F. Richardson

Guernica Editions Inc.
1241 Marble Rock Rd., Gananoque, (ON), Canada K7G 2V4
2250 Military Road, Tonawanda, N.Y. 14150-6000 U.S.A.
www.guernicaeditions.com

Distributors:
University of Toronto Press Distribution (UTP)
5201 Dufferin Street, Toronto (ON), Canada M3H 5T8
Independent Publishers Group (IPG)
814 N Franklin Street, Chicago, IL 60610, U.S.A.

First edition.
Printed in Canada.

Legal Deposit – First Quarter
Library of Congress Catalogue Card Number: 2025944298
Library and Archives Canada Cataloguing in Publication
Title: Catastrophilia / Julie Roorda.
Names: Roorda, Julie, author
Series: Essential poets ; 320.
Description: Series statement: Essential poets series ; 320
Identifiers: Canadiana 20250255561 | ISBN 9781778490149 (softcover)
Subjects: LCGFT: Poetry.
Classification: LCC PS8585.O683 C38 2026 | DDC C811/.6—dc23

For David

Table of Contents

The Art of Memory

the shore of Lake Ontario
        on the hinge of the Winter Solstice
                the horizon is a line of queuing ships

entering the Welland Canal
        to rise lock by lock and foil
                Niagara's inevitable flow

did you know Nikola Tesla's
        alternating current motor
                was inspired by Goethe's Faust

who longed for wings
        to follow the sun at dusk
                and become eternity

like the body of a dragonfly
        the crease in a symmetry
                of past and future

        imagine and remember
        they're the same thing

the same motion as a stone
        skipped once twice a thousand
                times across the surface

before slipping into time
        washing eventually back to the beach
                with ever shifting edges

Look: when you're mapping a coastline
        the smaller your unit of measurement
                the longer the coastline gets

Giordano Bruno's memory theatre
was more than a mnemonic device
it was a technique

for training the imagination
to dip into all knowledge
everything that ever was or will be

the Akashic records squirrelled beneath
the right forepaw of the Sphinx

the Egyptian word for beauty
is a lute the hieroglyph
for which combines symbols

of both sound and silence
wave / particle particle / wave
desire is the link

between essence and existence
the mystical love that is the loss
of subjectiveness

upon seeing Diana's beauty
Actaeon was turned into a stag
and consumed by his own dogs

the hunter become prey
the world in its unity

Love transforms and changes
into the thing that is loved he said
as the flames rose around him

and Bruno became the sun

Cat's Eye

The same year that Bruno burned,
German shoemaker Jakob Boehme perceived
in a glint of sunlight reflected
from a pewter water jug, the answer
to the problem of evil:
God, like Jung, would rather
be whole than good.

I've seen that same glint
in the eyes of my cat, whose gaze
interrogates the world with two
contradictory urges:
　　　　can I kill it?
　　　　can I sleep on it?
There you have it, the wholeness of Cat,
coincidence of comfort and wrath.

No wonder zealous witch-burners
used cats for kindling to spark
the thousands of bonfires that only confirmed
how goodness blazes brightest
in the grip of darkest night.

Though he was censored and condemned
from the pulpit, though his children
were bullied and his livelihood threatened,
Boehme, at least, had no fiery death.

Instead, he met glory at the feet
of his neighbours, offering a simple
glass of water, as he bent
to stitch their torn soles.

Catastrophilia

No mere rubber-necking
fascination with disaster,
rather, that deep-seated dread
that is a kind of hope, for release,
for significance. Meaning,
after all, is a backward glance.
When she heard the blasts, Lot's wife
remembered – the knowledge
was in her DNA: *I've been here before,*
and though her daughters screamed
to stop her, she looked back, just as Orpheus
turned to Eurydice: to witness the verge,
flashing luminous, where being merged
with non-being, time's eternal return.

Boreal Book of the Dead

Watersnake Mound
like the pyramids comprises
both tomb and text
the word-picture hieroglyphs
that read themselves
aloud in the dark
a snake is the word for life
and also depicts a walking stick
snake being the spoken sound
while the stick is the instrument
for etching it in the ground

the word for green
is spelled with things
that are green in different ways
moss fiddlehead garter snakes
the snake being the essence
of greenness which is newness
because it sheds its skin
a snake on a stick
becomes a caduceus
the wand of Hermes leading us
to and from
the land of the dead

the owl is the most common
image of a living thing
that signifies
its characteristic motion
which is knowing wisdom perception
the owl that can hear
its prey beneath
the surface of the earth
the word for death
is spelled with an owl

and a loaf of bread
the hunter
and the gathered

egret is the verb to tremble
ruffled by the wind that is all
that is left of a living thing
emptiness is the witness
unless your heart is light as a feather
at death expect to be devoured
by caiman-headed Ammut
rising hungry from the pond
it is not the pond that is bottomless
but the mud that lines its depth
buried you'll continue to fall

the word for swan
is both mother and death
a cygnet spells a fire-stick
that spins sparks out of air
and light into being
the death of the swan
rising in a gyre

watching the sky
is the way into the sky
from Hawk Hill highest
of the ridge of hillocks
deposited by a dying glacier
the best vantage for viewing
the seasonal migration of predators
of hawk-headed Horus
the watcher

seeing and shining
are the same thing
the moon the silver eye
that illumines
is both understanding

and what is understood
the verb to see is a sickle
to perceive
is a prayer shawl
together they form the boat
that ferries you
across the universe

Nocturne

Whistler spent most of the 1880s
painting on tiny wooden panels,
but I prefer to etch the undersides
of my eyelids, strictly private
nocturnes in black and gold,
luminous with bright spectres
and shimmering shadow forms.
The revolutionary art of closing
your eyes to see, and if you must
choose your frames of reference
for this or that, for the moment,
at least hold in mind: diaphanousness,
the light/dark sameness of outline
and the very space between.

Cat Versus Christmas Tree

Hard to tell them apart: both ancient, pagan, *sharp*.
Both dreaming of a forest, the tranquility of Eden,
branches mirroring roots in fearful symmetry,
craving chaos. These boughs once held candles,
dangerous sparks that now gleam, not in tinsel,
but in the green of the adversary's eyes. No,
he won't be thwarted by low branches
left strategically bare of shiny bulbs and loops.
He'll climb, for knowledge of good and evil
was always high-hanging fruit. No doubt,
there will be wreckage, havoc, a shifting pole,
the whole bright world come crashing down,
baubles and gifts crushed and scattered, and fallen.
But Tabby will have satisfaction,
    and Saturn the requisite sacrifice
    to herald the return of the Sun.

Conjuring Alice

1.

My grandmother taught me how to sit.
We come from a long line of sitters, she said,
but it takes much more than blood.

She was born in Lily Dale, in upstate New York.
where she was trained up from birth:
            it takes practice, discipline, work.

And so I sat, long and hard, scolded
when my attention faltered, or when I cried.
When I told her I was so bored I could hear myself growing,
            she smiled, and made me sit longer

still, until one day the chair
became an opening,
            an oubliette
            in the floor of my mind,

yes, yes, she whispered,
that's it, in order to remember,
you must first forget.

2.

I fall in a spiral, the torsional pull
of exploding consciousness,
            a whirligig of tickertapes
                        too speedy to decipher

more than flickers of non-sense,
                        I can see the wind here

I can read its intentions
regarding leaves, or a house in Kansas,
and the parade of faces, faces of ladies riding by,
their following eyes, be careful – if you can see them,
          they can see you,
          even inside your mind.

When the twister releases the crown
          of my head, I gyrate back widdershins
                    till I'm sitting again, exactly where I am,

and I ask my grandmother, *What happened?*

3.

Her great-grandmother knew the Fox sisters
whose haunted cottage was dismantled and shipped to Lily Dale,
over lake and land, to be reassembled, though it later burned down.

But weren't they exposed as hoaxers, I asked.
          How my grandmother laughed!

That night in my bedroom
the knocking began.

One-two-three is the call.
          The journey begins with refusal
                    but the call always wins.

Lake Erie has a powerful undertow,
the drag of the Falls, lure of the liminal,
no guarantee you'll survive the plunge

innocuous as the invitation may seem:
"Come for tea and table-tilting"

Alice Liddell, Ada Lovelace, Emma Hardinge Britten

I come from a long line of sitters.
I was eleven.

4.

Three-times-three
is nine knocks and you're in
admitted to the borderland.

She considered herself an ambassador
ferrying secrets between states of being
in diplomatic pouches:
          such were her crystals and cards.

Top secret was her scrying stone
of gleaming black obsidian.

She taught me Swedenborg's theory of correspondences:
everything we touch has otherworldly resonance
every action an interaction.

Magic number forty-two
is the twenty-first trump,
the World, times two,
divided by a looking glass
whose Janus glance takes in
both the seer and the seen.

5.

You too are two, she warned,
          Light Twin / Dark Twin, never apart.

If you attempt to reject the dark one
          you'll haunt yourself for the rest of your life.

Stare, stare until you see the scar
that casts half your face in shadow,

then knock three times on your own heart
            and allow yourself to enter,

you must learn to recognize yourself in the dark,
find the back of your own head and follow.

6.

All the dear dead await your appearance.
they've been waiting for you forever.

Do you mean it's the dead
who are conjuring us? I ask.
            The answer, of course, is yes.

            Vainly in dreams I sought you,
            said Beatrice to her Dante.

We are the ghosts, and always among them, both
of us imbued with luminiferous ether,
            the substance of all things,

a substance that is not material at all,
but merely the Will to Be.

7.

My grandmother's grave
            is marked by a white stone
                        etched with the name that only she knows,

and placed at the crossroads,
guarded by Hecate,
portal to the underworld, Hades,
            and its two eternal wells:
            Lethe and Mnemosyne.

Forget and remember,
you'll never fall into the same well twice.

When I gaze in the mirror
my grandmother looks back.
Who in the world am I? Alice asks.
I wonder if I've been changed in the night.

Triskelion

Of all the fledgling vegetables
in the garden, the rabbits prefer
the furled promise of fiddleheads,
their hidden cognition.

The mystery of the three hares:
they share only three ears,
yet each of them has two.

Circling endlessly,
a galaxy, a wormhole,
a snail occulted in its shell.

The drifting quality of perception.

The alchemist rabbit in the moon
magicking by mortar and pestle
that most elusive elixir.

Fibonacci discovered
his eponymous sequence
by observing rabbit reproduction:
nature's spiral signature,
the fractal by which everything grows.

It's a trick, isn't it?
Bursting from a black top hat,
wearing a waistcoat?

And we're always running late.

Yet spring returns, maddening.
The rabbits glean again
the garden's bounty,

spirit it away.

Shapeshifting

Consider Paracelsus' Doctrine of Signatures
whereby the form of all natural objects
may be read as sacred text or symbol
revealing their essential use: in 1691
an eighty-year-old Swedish werewolf
named Thiess of Kaltenbrun was put on trial
for heresy, flogged and banished for life
for trying, the judges decreed, to turn
people away from Christianity.
Thiess protested that he was, in fact,
a Hound of God, who entered Hell
to challenge the Devil, upon transforming
by virtue of the magic herb yarrow
whose stalks resemble the wolf's bushy tail.
Paracelsus would have believed him:
the doctor known as the Luther of Physicians
contended that empathy – union
with animal, vegetable or mineral –
is the principal means of acquiring knowledge,
the human being containing in microcosm
all constituents of the world.

Threshold

I woke up stranded
on a high-rise crane,
with rush hour below,
and the terror of where
did I think I was going?
I was joined by a seagull
to whom I explained fear
of heights, and ambition.
Nonsense, the seagull said,
Failure is the test, and flew off.
The wind picked up,
the fire trucks arrived.
        I went back to sleep
        and fell into the sky.

Amazement

we decided to walk the maze
in High Park but got lost on our way
through the dogs off-leash area
we'd been told to follow
Anubis the dog-headed god
but nobody told us what breed
I thought the Great Dane
but you followed the Basset Hound
which meant we moved
at very different speeds
and got separated
and when we finally found
each other again your ears
were muddy from drooping
so close to the ground
I cleaned them with mugwort
which gave you clairaudience
and after that you wouldn't listen
to a word I said
shushed me for interrupting
the voices of the dead
so I said why don't you ask
the dead how to find the maze
but that would require an offering
something symbolic like a feather
so we headed for the duck pond
which we were told to find
by following a trail of bread crumbs
but the crumbs had been snapped up
by Ibis-headed Thoth and we wound
up by the burial mounds
feeling very hungry
I ate some deadly nightshade
which gave me clairvoyance
so I could see the dead beneath our feet
they invited us in and between us

my eyes and your ears
we could communicate nicely
but they told us being dead
isn't all it's made out to be
and suggested we consult the oracular
capybara so we set out for the zoo
we were told we could find
directly aligned with the Belt
of Orion but the llamas blocked us
said we must prove ourselves first
but the only way to do so
was to find our way out
of the maze we had yet to find

So Below

I would become a tree
to expand as naturally above
ground as below
spanning sky and underworld
equivalently
to live and die and live
to feed munching worms
with bright foliage
I used to pity Daphne
imprisoned by her fight
to be free
now I see it is a gift

I would climb into a tree
as a coffin
read the *ars moriendi*
inscribed in its bark
and sung by its roots
like a dirge
did you know that thirsty
trees scream ultrasonically
the coffin becomes
a canoe for the crossing
river of life
river of death
the way is the way

Flying Ointment

You'll recognize it by its leaves
like wizened old hands: clary sage,
whose tincture smudged on your eyelids
will endow you with lucidity, with faery sight,
and sibylline dreams, and you'll begin
to see the blue edges of everything,
and finally take flight with the phantom
armies, the furious Ladies of the Night
and their witchy familiars: the cats
and the owls, the wolves and the bats,
all led by Diana on that wildest of hunts,
merry and macabre, through the bedrooms
of mortals to the dark side of the moon,
where you'll howl back at the earth and laugh!

Weird Sisters

datura
dilates pupils
inducing night-vision
inviting dark in
to become datura is to turn
into a black dog
Cerberus
guarding the underworld

henbane
grown in graveyards
becomes the crown
of Hercules
by which he travels
to Hades
and from
in its cauldron-shaped pod
you may become
a door

vervain
must be gathered with the left
hand at the rising
of the Dog Star Sirius
to protect infants
from theft by fairies
a hand chopped
from a hanged man and dried
by a fire of vervain
will render its holder
invisible

wormwood
harvested on Hallowe'en
becomes ink sending words
to the dead
inscribed on flakes
of papyrus and placed
in the mouth
of a corpse
its poison preserves
the missive
from worms

mandrake
is spawned by semen
of a hanged man
a fertility charm
its humanoid root
must be harvested
by a black dog
for its screams
at being wrenched
from the earth become
fatal to the gatherer
or as Theophrastus taught
you may dig up mandrake
safely with a sword
if you talk continuously
of love

The Belled Buzzard of Genoa

Every bad omen can be traced back
to a nasty little childhood prank,
like a sheep bell knotted around the neck
of an unlucky turkey vulture
whose un-heard-of bird-life-span
means no one is safe, not yet, not ever.
(Did I mention it was eighteen-seventy-four?)
Nor geography for reports have spread
across Europe and around the entire world
of its sharp shadow passing in front of the sun.
If you see it, block your ears to its fateful din
the clarion call that portends the worst.
It's likely too late, if you've already heard,
but if the buzzard of Genoa flies overhead
          whatever you do,
          do not play dead.

The Oracle Applies for EI

Fear and persecution, she could have borne;
cast like Jeremiah into a miry cistern, fine.

But once millennials transferred faith
to apps and algorithms, and complained

that it was inconvenient to pay by sacrifice
of goats or bullocks or turtle-doves,

she knew it was time. Never mind
her spectacular success rate, her firm refusal

to tell clients only what they wanted to be true,
and so many glowing testimonials to her skill,

obtained, necessarily, from beyond the grave.
She even branched out into motivational speaking:

The Power of Negative Thinking.
Many of her forebears were oracles,

but never before has the scale of impending disaster
been so immense. Imagine how you would feel

subjected daily to visions of catastrophe,
collective and personal, doomed to befall

every single customer who dings your bell.
Hence, the attached medical diagnosis:

*Pre-*Traumatic Stress Disorder,
(the flash-forwards are the worst)

and a special request that her application
be processed promptly,

before the apocalypse.

The Haunting, 1963

Before Prozac, there were poltergeists.
Stone spoke to the lonely. Close walls
scrawled love letters, secretly, in the night;
stairways offered rare invitation to dance,

and the dark halls called out sweet nothings.
Must longing render its object delusion,
deem hungerer hysterical, ridiculous, shrill?
Am I crazy, or is this real? Yes. *Yes.*

My love may be unrequited by the known
laws of the familiar universe, but truth
is for transgressors. And even you, Doctor,
cannot deny the universal reality of desire.

For I will enter through open gates
while the rest return to their dreams.

Frya's Watch

thirty years after it left Earth
and approached interstellar space
Voyager 2 began transmitting back data

in an unknown language
scientists did not understand:
echo after echo of the Big Bang
the First Word given by Wralda,
Originating Spirit, to the ancient Frisians,
the goddess Frya's children

and the only language in which,
according to the Oera Linda Book, one can
understand what it means to be free

Bergson's *élan vital* requires a continual increase
of freedom and novelty, an infinite number of stars,
eternity of incarnations

after all, if life's concern was merely adaptation
we'd all just be thriving amoebas, wouldn't we?
Contained, no drive toward complexity, or individuation
and no need surely to die

Better to be dead than a slave
are the words inscribed on a monument
to the Battle of Warns
in 1345 in which the Frisians repelled
the Dutch from the eastern coast of the Zuider Zee

Frya taught her children not to tolerate the unfree,
neither those who would enslave others
nor those who would sell their own souls

but freedom, like nether lands
reclaimed again and again over millennia
from the ever-encroaching seas demands vigilance

Read, learn and stand guard
cries Frya from her watch-star spark
of perpetual fire, words recorded for posterity
on paper pressed from the leaves
of red-tinted water lilies

Afterlife.com

Cyberlimbo teems with the ghosts
of those who've forgotten their passwords.
What *was* Mother's maiden name?
What about the dog that ran away?

No matter. History is redundant
once you pass through the faux-pearl gates
of Disney Heaven, to which your profile
may be transmitted by facsimile. No ID required.

What a relief to be released from memory-
laced muscle, earthly remains mere carbon-
capture vessels, breath of life exhaled
as fine particulate ash. What a blast!

In the end, flesh becomes The Word™.
You too can live forever.

Snakes and Ladders

John Dee, known as the most learned man in Europe
had a library of more than four thousand books:
          Euclid to Copernicus,
          Calvin to Koran.

He was the model for Shakespeare's Prospero,
having conjured the tempest that gave Elizabeth Rex
victory over the Spanish, and an Empire.

A trusted spy, the original 007,
which was not a number but a glyph
depicting two eyes shaded by four fingers,
thumb splayed beside his face –
'twas how he signed his secret missives.

Like Einstein he sought
a unified field of harmonious wisdom
distilled of the full diversity
of Renaissance thought:
          the Great Work

which he mapped upon a Ouija board,
the snapping, sparking circuitry
          of the mind of God

whereby he learned the revelation of Eden,
enlightenment of all creation
two trees:
          life and knowledge
          ladder and snake

the sinewy winding path of face to face
taught to him by angels.

Or were those demons speaking
through the sorcerer's stone
the vapours of the crucible?

Such accusations started early,
levelled first when the student Dee crafted
a real flying machine
for a stage production of Aristophanes' Peace.

Next he was jailed by Bloody Mary
on charges of enchantment,
and had he not been championed by her sister
he might have met an early, tortured death.

Even at the height of his success,
rumours of devil-dabbling persisted,
flourished under the witch-hater James.

And, as if to prove the judgement
of mere humans
is anathema to wisdom

Dee's days ended in poverty
and ridicule, forced to sell his books
        one-by-one
        in exchange for food.

A Spider's Worth

Spiders are useful bugs, my mother said.
They spin webs that serve a purpose,
ridding the world of use-less flies.
It was a distinction I did not grasp:
couldn't you say it was the flies that served
a purpose by being food? What I did perceive
was the excessive elegance of eight legs
and the fabulous architecture of their webs,
which were not all teleology, spanning footpaths
at dawn, bush to bush, as if they could not help
but spew silver all night long, too fragile to catch
anything, but stopping me up just the same
with their touch, scrabbling at my face to brush
away their invisible yet indelible trace.

The Fool

It might have been a dream,
a vague voice, a mere whisper
that was really a wish
for a role to play, for importance:
    Take down Ninevah! That seat of empire,
    idolatry, and brutal cruelty.

But then Jonah woke up and saw clearly
– more prophet he –
    that such wickedness
    is rarely punished.

The ordeal would be entirely his:
    Three days and nights
    in the belly of the fish.

For Ninevah, far from being destroyed
in forty days, was spared,

and Jonah, left a fool,
scarred and ridiculous.
I do well to be angry, he complained to God,
    angry enough to die.

And can you blame him
for wanting the wrath of heaven
to rain down on them,
for wanting it to end.
    Wouldn't you rather be Cassandra,
    unheeded, but always right?

But prophecy can be a very long game
and Ninevah did get its comeuppance
-- a century after Jonah's death –

to the satisfaction of a lucky three,
more timely seers,
Isaiah, Zephaniah, Nahum.

Fools and their dreams.
All according to God's plan.

Sunlight Mysteries

Charles Fort, historian
of the anomalous, spent years,
in the New York Public Library,
collating thousands of reports
of phenomena exceeding the limits
of twentieth-century reason:
trails of giant footprints,
showers of flinty stones,
floating cities, luminous owls,
waterfalls reversing their flow,
spontaneous combustion in creatures
as various as porpoises and priests –
a vast array of extraordinary true-stories
damned to obscurity though witnessed
by scores of ordinary people –
elaborating as he did a new mental structure
able to recognize as real the real-life
intermediaries between positive-negative,
particle-wave, literal-metaphor,
living-dead, a Philosophy of the Hyphen,
uniting all things in the truth-fiction
that there are no stable distinctions
only relations, the coincidence
of meaninglessness to express
the hilarity of ultimate Oneness.

Alien-Big-Cats and Women-in-Black

there's always something off about them, hoaxer, spectral,
or unhinged, then there are the creepy children at your door
strongly seeking permission to enter, though fear will suffice
in lieu of invitation and when the door opens find
they have no whites-of-their-eyes only chasms of dark
and the hackles on the back of your neck will rise
but that's just the start of the high strangeness, suddenly
the building is completely empty, except for the librarian,
there's always a librarian, and reports of black panther
corpses disappearing from villages in England
that begin with B: Battersea, Barnsley, Blackburn, Bath,
think what you like, but however these Imposters
plead or inveigh, do not let them
whisk your wee ones away.

The Wisdom of Anomalies

The mandate of the Fluke Institute for Improbability Research
is to investigate outliers, logic-defiers and uncommon sense,

the deviant data discarded by scientists who conform
to the tunnel-vision of accepted theory.

No more chasing the averages, medians and middling patterns
of predictability that leach the life out of genuine explorers.

Look past the merely plausible to the spectacular vacillations
of the actual, the multi-faceted spectrum of possibility.

Paradox, irony and absurdity are of particular interest
as they crack the causal chains of consensus reality

to elicit the surprise synchronicities of meaning.
Inquiries currently underway at the Fluke include the following:

Does a rain of anchovies on a remote Italian village
confirm the superiority of a Mediterranean diet?

Is alliteration the secret behind the Squamish sasquatch sightings?
Will the blue moon usher in an era of aesthetic revolution?

Are mothmen munching holes in the fabric of the universe?
Established by a generous donor, who wished to be known

only by the fact that she survived three strikes by lightning
– before succumbing to a chunk of falling space junk

that split her skull – the Fluke Institute is devoted to opening minds
and disseminating the fruits of serious serendipity.

This Is Your Life

Having trouble finding yourself? Too multi-tasked
to trace the story you so famously need to live?
Listen: narrative is dead. Probability is the new imperative,
With TruYu Analytics your every move will elicit a 99%
accurate prediction for next and future steps. For example:
your recent choice of spray-foam versus roll-on insulation
predicts an 85% chance of marital infidelity within the year;
voting for the incumbent will reduce your risk of tennis elbow
by nearly a third; and every time you buy ice cream the threat
of death by shark attack rises 8%. Every choice fosters
a feedback loop that will eventually eliminate any need at all
for decision-making, consternation about perceived missteps,
and, ultimately, guilt, which is not to say you won't be held
responsible, punished or made to pay, but with TruYu
comes this assurance: you will always be yourself.
Isn't that, after all, what the story is all about?

Ascent

Before she was committed to the flames,
Marguerite Porete was sentenced to watch
the book for which she was condemned
publicly burned, and was invited to renounce
the work to spare her body the same fate.
Solitary and itinerant Marguerite had been accused
of espousing the Heresy of the Free Spirit
that was so alarming to the church
for its currency among women
who sloughed off convention and sought
divine perfection in this life, uncloistered.
Her *Mirror of Simple Souls*, a dialogue
between Knowledge and Love,
describes seven stages of spiritual progress
in the soul's ascent to God.
Written in French instead of lofty Latin,
the text's popularity was widespread,
and try as they might, the inquisitors
could not destroy every copy.
Perhaps that's why she could refuse so calmly
to recant, but chose instead to cherish
the content of the pages quickly consumed
by flames, knowing that, returned to ash,
words are indistinguishable from flesh.

The Magician

She died on his thirty-seventh birthday,
a vial of mercury

their only child.

It was his first sight of her
that had confirmed his belief
that divinity permeates matter.

The soul, he said, is a royal essence
that only leaves the court to see the country.

She undoubtedly a queen.

They didn't just see it, they lived it,
the primordial urge of creation,

alchemy as a verb:
Love was their laboratory,
the crucible, her beauty.

How could he have known
the little death
at the threshold of union,

when the soul slips
the body momentarily, then returns,

was not enough?

How could he have forgotten
that Mercury is a thief?

He continued to sign every work
with both their names, until his own
death eight years later,

at the hand of that same trickster,
messenger of the gods.

The chemical wedding
of Thomas and Rebecca Vaughan:

Eros and death collapsing time
to the single point, from which all
of creation ever expands,

the Big Bang,
love as potential, whose true

attainment is love.

Trickster

After years of dreaming
of coyotes, the Trickster appears
in my path, hurtling towards me.
But by now I've recessed
flight and fight, and evolved
to exegesis: the ability to discern
in animate being, the vision I've foreseen.
This is key. A true symbol
participates in its own reality.
Like teeth tearing into the jugular
to reveal a gurgling blood-bright stream
of consciousness. These are common
mistakes: substance for illusion,
and vice versa, and that's exactly
          what I mean, coyote says,
          so close I can smell his fetid breath.

Anxiety

I would trust
the coyotes in High Park
harbour no desire
to harm, but knowing
they can smell fear
terrifies me.

I can only strive
for the ease
of these frontier-thrivers
unleashed, assured,
feet in two worlds

and covet their conviction,
graced with the gift
of prophecy
that will always, at least,
foresee dinner.

Provoked by my
odorous heresies,
no doubt,
they'd make short work
of this faithless hide.

But don't worry,
they'll hiss, ripping in
to my thin disguise:
this is the beginning
of wisdom.

A sudden sprouting of wings

Night after night
my unconscious casts up visions
of apocalypse, the latest episode
featuring a gigantic, rampaging
Godzilla-like monster
named Owen.
I only know one Owen.
He's a television character,
a brute, who recently told off
his daughter's ex-boyfriend,
father of his grandchild,
who also happens to be his
(ie. Owen's) girlfriend's son
(the boyfriend, not the grandchild)
for being a *useless waste of space*.
Well. Isn't that a soap opera-
worthy coupling
of symbols: creature
capable of laying waste
to civilization vis-à-vis
my nagging suspicion
that I'm wasting my time.
Archetypal terror mis-
matched to minor
failure.
(Was St. John, too,
just having trouble
getting published?)
Maybe it has something to do
with it being New Year's.
Maybe (and this may be a stretch),
it has something to do with the fact
that the title of my latest flop
includes a frog. Not quite a reptile,
like Owen, but close.

Amphibian, double-natured,
living both on water
and on land.
There was a shore.
And as I fled Owen's
calamitous advance
along the coastline
I briefly considered whether
I might find refuge
in the sea.
On second thought,
Owen's advantage over me
only multiplied in water,
given his approximately
12-metre height.
I had to turn inland.
But while water is said
to represent emotion,
what is land in the land-
scape of the psyche?
Intellect? Wit?
Oh, what does it matter,
I could never outrun him.
My only hope
could come from above:
rescue by helicopter, or –
what the heck,
this is a dream –
a sudden sprouting of wings.
But then I remember
another night's version
in which I escape waves
of aircraft dropping from the sky,
or rather, I wake,
which is not the same
as escape at all.
Just the catastrophe
of morning.
Day after day.

Post-Heresy

Long before Christianity
calcified into code of Empire,
Origen of Alexandria pursued divine gnosis
with such urgency, he castrated himself
to avoid distraction. Applying the tools
of his neo-Platonist education,
he read the gospel analogically, a story
of every soul's destiny: the return to God,
a pilgrimage that might encompass
several incarnations, in various bodies.
He believed salvation to be universal:
even the devil would be redeemed
by the end of time, (a magnanimous
position, given the ongoing terror
and persecution to which he was subjected).
God, he said, had better
things to do than torture souls for eternity.
Driven finally to flee to Palestine,
he found no safety. When an outbreak
of the plague was blamed on Christian magic,
he was imprisoned, beaten, and died
of his wounds shortly after his release.
And only three centuries after his death,
Origen had the great distinction
of being declared a heretic
by the Second Ecumenical Council
of Constantinople, by which time
his soul had transmigrated, and was soaring,
winged, high above wisdom's dome.

The Hanged Man

If wrestling with demons could improve
muscle tone, my shoulders would grow wings.

I've enrolled in a local night-flight school,
also called Knowledge of Good and Evil.

The Fall was always my favourite. Trick-or-treating
and cavities. Give us this Day of the Dead.

To confirm my identity, I'll have to consult
dental records. Meanwhile, there's the waiting room.

Anticipation is a common squirrel affliction.
Twitch twitch twitch twitch twitch twitch twitch.

The best way to count the nuts on the ground
is to hang upside-down from the tree.

Sky Burial

According to Plato, the soul,
in its original state, was feathered,
which is why its awakening
begins with an all-over prickling
sensation, the goosebumps
that apprehend truth. I'd rise up
a raven. Ravens prefer glistening
things, and where do I shine most,
but my eyes? Or a blue-black crow,
ever in company of a clatter of kindred
souls. Better yet, a hawk, my cracked
old heart held aloft on razor-sharp claws.
            And all that is left transformed
            by carrion butterflies.

Soul Carrier

Someone hurled a beer bottle
at a swan overnight and she floats
dead now, on the pond

like a discarded wedding dress,
while her mate feeds nearby,
inscrutable as the rising sun.

Standing on the shore, I feel like the subject
of the ancient Egyptian poem,
"A Man Tired of Life in Dispute with His Soul,"

who argues in favour of death,
for living, the man pleads,
is destroying him.

The pyramids at Giza, like archaic monuments
worldwide, align with the stars
of the constellation Cygnus, the Swan

symbol of transformation and grace,
psychopomp to the Greeks,
meaning "soul-carrier."

The purpose of the monuments so designed,
is to direct the soul, at the moment of death,
to the fork in the Milky Way

that marks the entrance to the passage, called variously
River of Souls, the Way of Birds, the Ghost Road,
that returns the illuminated spirit

and all its accumulated wisdom, to its Source.

In the poem, the man's soul argues back
that life is the sacrifice that precedes awakening,
it is the nature of becoming.

Go ahead and hang up your misery,
Soul says, *but that hook*
belongs to me.

The reason for the man's particular agony
is unknown, described only as despair
at the degenerate state of society.

Well, nothing changes, and changes everything,
the daily battle: Light, edged by the clouds of dawn
tinted pink with the blood of the swan,

emerges from darkness. And my soul
admonishes me to love the waking world,
this heaven become hell, becoming heaven.

Alice's Daisy Chain

Daisies are unique
among flowers.
They always have 13,
or 21,
or 34 petals,
three Fibonacci
numbers in sequence.
The higher you go,
the closer
two numbers
divided by each other,
approach the golden ratio,
recipe for perfect beauty,
wormhole
to infinity.

Rosicrucian novitiates
were blindfolded,
then instructed to chase
a white rabbit
deep underground,
to a great hall, beneath
a tall mountain,
to face a trial
of initiation.

The most common scene
in Egyptian art
is the weighing, on scales,
of the human heart
against a feather of truth.
There are 42 crimes
that must be denied,
and the last, the oldest
rule in the book?

No, your honour, I swear,
I did not steal the tarts!

According to physics
It takes 42 minutes
for an object to fall
through the middle
of the earth

but would such a trip
be up or down,
and how high
would it fall
once it rose
from the ground?

On Making Your Life Agree with the Heavens

The word desire
is derived
from the Latin
desiderare
meaning "from the stars,"
yet when I stand
at the highest
point in High Park,
chosen precisely to be
closest to the sun
when it finally slips
above the horizon,
I could swear
that the longing
flows out, *from* me.
No wonder
Marsilio Ficino
was called Psychotherapist
of the Renaissance;
the purpose
of his manual
of star magic
was not to foresee
earthly events,
but to reflect
the soul's qualities back
to the self, a game
of mirrors to guide
the spirit's ascent,
flying toward God
as God flies
toward all things.

Absence

I'm forever losing the baby on the subway,
and realizing – worse than concrete, tiled tunnels,
pinched train doors – the more substantial barrier
to her retrieval is consciousness, the evolution
of which is to become aware of the undetectable,
every sense striving for a breach: scanning
for tiny opalescent hands reaching through
sidewalk grates, sniffing fluffs of her hair
blown from a dandelion blooming in asphalt.
Have you ever noticed how much a nattering
squirrel sounds like a newborn's cry?
It is only by the force of loss, its bottoming pull
    that we may infer the existence
    of dark matter, otherwise unseen,
    the very longing that holds
    the entire universe in being.

Sudden Dark

after Dante Gabriel Rossetti

I have been here before,
But where you are I do not know;
You're always just beyond a door
Where I can't go,
Though longing for you howls from every pore.

You have been mine before –
How many times I cannot tell.
Eternally did I adore
And hold you well,
Till now; your absence haunts my very core.

Will time our love restore,
Before this incarnation's night?
Or must I struggle to death's shore
'Fore we unite,
And day and night yield one delight once more?

Entanglement

Love, I missed my timeshift cue
            and you have slipped further away.

The clue?

It must have been the crow
with the strand of blood red wool
in its beak. I just watched it fly
to the top of the cell tower,
            failed to take vital heed.

Why do ravel and unravel
mean the same thing?

It's the Law of Penelope:
once two souls interact
they display internal correlation
regardless of their relevant position
in time and space.

            She ties a knot, Ulysses sails.

Spooky action at a distance.
The White Queen screams.

I'll feel the pain soon,
and soon, and soon again,
severance by a thousand pinpricks.

You're hidden from me
beneath this space-time shroud.
I can't shout loud enough to reach you.
I can't find you in my sleep

But watch the birds, Love,
            their choreography
that holds the very world in being
and we'll touch each other again
(and soon again)
woven tightly
                    tangle free.

Unhinged

The charge:
enchantment.

I couldn't deny it.

All those times I was seen
leaving the house after dark.

Of course I was flying,
I was on my way to you!

A journey lit by corpse candles,
flickering
Will o' the Wisps.

Did you know each wisp
must lure one traveller astray
for every day of the year

to win a chance to lead
the devil's stagecoach?

But who bewitched whom
when we contrived our hidden bed
and discovered Plato's heresy:

before the Fall,
male and female
were one.

Two faces fixed upon a round neck,
eight limbs entwined,
one soul and mind.

We could see everything!
Even in the dark, especially then,
knowledge of good *and* evil;

desire, the hinge.

The gods understood
that unity was a threat.

The sentence: severance.

Life after life longing
to possess our other half,
to recollect.

We remembered,
and once again

a neck was snapped.

Magicicada

In Lundy's Lane Cemetery,
I hear the first cicada of the summer,
now a second, and a third.
Caspar, Balthasar and Melchior,

offering in triparte chorus, a song
of wisdom hard-won: a thirteen-year
transformation by imaginal cells,
winged fantasies.

Mere nymph to full-blown flier
and skilled musician, entire body
a lyre like that of Orpheus
serenading the short journey
back to the underworld.

We rise by which we fall,
this is the ladder of alchemy,
angels ever travelling up and down.

I used to wear the cicadas' shed skins
like merit badges, hooking their clever ghost
claws to the weave of my shirt

and Lundy's Lane was once the site
of a famous battle, in the only real war:
the struggle for borderland.

Life after life, in the quest
for individuality, we delineate
our separate skins,
only to relinquish them
again and again.

Twilight Sleep

it's about willingness to take risk
the radical trust of the poppy flaming
and dying in a single season, survives
by the wings of a bee, willingness to risk
ambiguity, like perennial belladonna
as well-acquainted with the underworld
as with the sun sigilled in starry calyces
black jewels of deathly sweet fruit
a concoction of the two was administered
during childbirth to ease the transition
between worlds, not just the pain but the memory
of pain, the transforming power of forgetting
          what you don't remember
          must be lived

The Measure of the Fish

A tombstone of polished granite
etched with the image of a fisherman
casting a fly rod.

Another carved with the symbolic
Vesica Piscis containing the Greek
word for fish, which is also an acronym
drawn from a prophecy of the Erythraean Sibyl,

interpreted by Augustine
to mean the One Without Sin,
whose birth into the abyss called mortality
was marked by the conjunction
of Saturn and Jupiter in the sign of two fishes
swimming in opposite directions,
joined by a yoke.

This plow the driving force
for the coming of consciousness.

In his first known miracle the child Jesus
cast out salt from a dried sardine
and restored it to life
setting it free in a stream.

Pythagoras' "measure of the fish," the intersection
of two circles, meant the joining of two worlds
in a dyad, reflection, the first manifestation
that gave birth to the entire universe.

Also seen in Gothic Arches,
the Womb of Mary, and the Madorla of Venus:
portals all.

Add a third circle and it becomes
the Flower of Life, or Fisherman's Net
known to ancients as a blueprint
for creation.

Recalled when Simon Peter drew
a net from the Sea of Galilee
near to bursting with fish

and each spring, in the village
of Yoro in Honduras
when a Rain of Fish falls, providing
a much-needed feast.

Scintilla

Earth's atmosphere diffracts
starlight unevenly
creating the appearance
          of twinkles.

This is deception
I can love, which raises
some questions about the nature of truth:

is truth lovable,
          or is lovable true,
however ephemeral? Does love ever

last – Janus-faced word,
meaning end and forever. Didn't that star die
long ago? A lasting good-bye,

those winks in the night, light trails
like eyelashes
          grazing my cheek.

Forms of Devotion

Simeon the Stylite spent thirty-seven years
in the desert on a small wicker platform atop a pillar,
its height extended to sixty feet as the very crowds
he sought to avoid gathered below and grew.

Alarmed, at first, by his spreading fame,
Simeon's superiors devised a test
of his true motivation:
                                        Order him to descend.
Should he spurn his vow of obedience and refuse –

exposing Pride – they would force him
violently down. But when, in Humility,
he complied, they halted his descent and ordered
him instead to remain.
                                        The suffering continued
to flock to the site of Simeon's sacrifice.
They passed up the minimum morsels of bread
and water required to live, handed down small pails
of excrement, knelt in the meager shade cast

by the column to swallow dust scraped from its stone
and thus, thousands were healed.

Corpse Position

On your back,
arms outstretched,
lower body raised
in a half-bridge,
an excellent metaphor
for the present collision
of life inevitably half-died,
half-lived. Or,
the Large Hadron Collider
firing opposing particle beams
at near light speed;
answers to every mystery
forthcoming. Still,
you will notice, you're still
breathing. When you squeeze
your knees tightly
to your chest,
your curved back
the hull of a drunken
little boat hurled to and fro,
try to stay clear
of the two-inch plunge
looming at the edge
of your mat. Falling
is the one fear we're born with;
rising the one with which
we die. Entwine
your knuckles behind your head,
let your bent knees fall
right while turning
to face the left.
Until 3000 years ago,
the brain's two hemispheres
functioned independently,
allowing us to perceive
voices emanating from the right

as those of the gods.
Since then, silence.
Now on hands and knees,
arch your back,
then reverse the curve,
belly down, and repeat.
Cat and cow, scary and sacred,
reverence and fear.
As a child you were terrified
you'd encounter your evil twin;
now you're just afraid
you'll meet the good one.
There are two halves to the numinous,
tail-in-mouth, the ouroboros,
Or, a cobra, eyes skyward,
trunk raised. Pipe-player
or snake – who
hypnotizes whom?
Resume corpse
position. Eyes closed,
palms splayed upward
as if in offering.
Good, you're good at this one.
Try not to fall asleep.
The knack for playing dead
is a sign of evolved being.

The View from Infinity

today the park is bathed
in the pale yellow light
peculiar to this city in October

yellow as pale as it can be
without being white, shift
between summer harsh and winter crisp

the shimmering veil
that separates – that is, gives shape –
to what's beyond

a well-known Near Death Experience
researcher who slipped out
of her hemorrhaging body

found herself in a void
with nothing but a sense of shimmer
from which she created a tree

before being suctioned back
into her body by the force
of a blood transfusion

today I am a woman looking up
from a hill, the highest ground
in Toronto's downtown

also an ancient burial site
a few kilometres to my right
the city's tallest spire

tomb of a different kind
as people only ascend that tower
to look down

it is this conjunction of opposites
that defines our existence
knowing and not-knowing

such was the revelation
to Nicholas of Cusa on the boat
trip back from Constantinople

where he'd tried to bridge
the gap between Eastern
and Western Christendom

which in the ongoing
absence of not-knowing
continues

today October lights a hemorrhage
of leaves, a red river
and it's nearly Hallowe'en

when the line between worlds
is less a veil than a mist
permeable if you've the courage

that is, the humility, Nicholas'
"learned ignorance," to enter, to become
void becoming shimmer

Stigmata

There is wild speculation how
the holy hermit fell pregnant –

it was the wind, it was the swamp,
it was a long-stemmed rose.

While the secret waxes visible
in belly and blush, guardian cats

thrust and parry, noses upheld
in an air of knowing. Dead saints

smell of lily and ambergris;
what is the scent of sainthood born?

Sweet blood-oranges and iron-cold
water from a desert stone.

Salvation swells within, still
supplicants trot out offerings

to the base of her mountain: pitted cherries,
pixie sticks, a wicked pack of cards.

They cross her palm with silver
nails, expecting deliverance, soliciting

signs of the time

11:11

It is the experience of coincidence
that is the engine of wonder and religious belief,
irrupting into our lives with the sheer absurdity of meaning.

Consider Arthur Koestler's Library Angel,
that shivery spirit tapping his shoulder
to draw attention to a perfect and timely text.

And yes! The very book I require
appears, this time in a cardboard box
abandoned by the curb: an ancient grimoire

elucidating all chains of chains and correspondence,
a medieval search engine called Sympathetic Magic,

for the ancients well knew
what the modern human interface
with burgeoning technology reveals
about the nature of consciousness:

the universe does not order information
like a cosmic card catalogue in time and space,
instead, we know nothing but that
          which we imagine ("the future")
          or remember ("the past")

knowledge traversed by patterns of association
meeting in an eternal now

where time is a circuit board of attention
looping in infinite directions
where everyday miracles are actually
the most rational of possible events.

Aquarius

Vernal equinox, and the hawk
has returned to its perch atop
the tower behind my house,

one of an imposing array that bear
high-voltage power lines away
from Niagara's turbines.

In our last encounter, it was autumn,
and the hawk tilted and dove toward its target:
a squirrel, unwitting, shucking a peanut
I had left for it on the back fence.

Horrified that I had laid that deadly trap,
I rushed out, flapping my arms
– my poor excuse for wings –
and chased the predator off.

That night, a dream: lightning
surging through the power lines,
crumpling the steel towers in a mangled heap,
and a wall of fire threatening to enter
the wide open back door,

an animal shriek rose through my solar
plexus, but I couldn't tell which one I was:
the hawk or the squirrel?

Apocalypse, or the dawn
of the Age of Aquarius crystallizes
the problem of the union of opposites

also known throughout history
as the Philosopher's Stone

No longer can evil be defined
as the mere absence of good,
or vice versa

and the Universe, in its infinite wisdom,
will conjure all the plagues of Egypt
if that's what it takes

for the Self to wake up
in this heaviest of dreams, the Earth,
and forge a new way.

The sixteenth century alchemist
Gerhard Dorn recognized that parallel

between the chemistry in the retort
and the moral transformation
of the human heart.

The Spirit Mercurius, the seed
of unity-in-chaos
can only be accomplished within
the individual.

Duality reimagined:
is this a cave wall or a mirror?
My shadow or my reflection?

Or is the only difference
between the two the direction
of the light?

Resistance

Today she would have been criticized
as foolish, impractical, not *goal-oriented.*
She sabotaged a promising career
to fight against Fascists in Spain,
but refused to fire any weapons.
She chose to share the fate of the oppressed
with backbreaking work on a farm
and in an auto factory, only to collapse
and be sent home with acute pleurisy.
And though she escaped the Nazis herself,
she restricted her own diet to the same
scant rations allowed her French compatriots
back home, thus hastening her own
early death. Simone Weil
did not exercise resistance
despite its futility, but because of it.
In an absurd world where good and evil
mix inextricably, the only goal
worth pursuing is, by definition, impossible.
The impossibility of pure and authentic
Goodness. The mystery. All the more
urgent the imperative to seek.

Judgement

A blast a thousand times the size
of that which flattened Hiroshima:
an asteroid? a black hole? an errant
chunk of antimatter? or the crash
of a nuclear-powered Martian craft,
igniting a crack in the fabric of space/
time, and our planet's fateful
swerve into the twentieth century?
No witnesses, only the aftermath.
(Were they coming to warn us?)
It is not enough to ask what happened,
Tunguska begs the deeper question:
        what if eighty million trees fall
        in the forest and nobody hears?

Exit pursued by a bear

(stage direction from Shakespeare's *The Winter's Tale*)

I would be the bear
and hope that when I left the earth
it would not be in fight or flight.

Callisto, pursued by gods,
lived sixteen years a bear
before she saw her name in lights:

Ursa Major, never to set or rise.
The soul is a bear in its infinite form
pillar around which the night sky flies.

Revolution fixed by rest, the contrary
stands firm, rendered stable
by its very contrariety.

The Winter's Tale: dead as a statue
for sixteen years, Hermione,
a secret inscribed in stone,

concealed – so Hermes promised
to Asclepius – for the future world
when some may seek that sacred wisdom,

reanimated at Paulina's words,
"Music, awake her," that of the spheres,
song of the Great Bear's return.

Atlantis Rising

Since the dawn of the Age
of Leo, over twelve thousand years ago,
the Falls have eroded eleven

kilometres from Queenston Heights,
carving a serpentine gorge in the rock
south to their current site, cut in two

one part curved like a lucky horseshoe, Niagara:
border city of bridal suites and barrels.
Ghosts abound by rushing water, ever-hazy
in perpetual mist.

It's Christmas

and the coloured light-show splayed
across the enormous ice eggs
beneath the flow reminds me

of the eerie blue-glow
of the terrible crystal,

Poseidia's power plant,
and its supercharged web
of firestones, god's eyes

(they called it progress then too,
the slavery of techno-trapped souls)

until its destruction fissured the earth
and it sank beneath the surf so long ago.
Do you remember?

The mad scramble for boats,
the scattering to the far-flung
shores of the earth,

me to Alexandria, you
to the Isle of Man –
            or was it the other way
                        around?

Why do we keep doing this,
keep longing for apocalypse,
for something that will change us
            so we don't have to?

Last night, coyotes howled
            in the hydro corridor out back
                        as we lay awake, huddled together

under the covers, and you shuddered
            and said, it sounds like a banshee,

            doesn't that herald a death?

Yes, Love, you see, in the realm
            of the trickster death is a test,
                        and by some cosmic sleight-of-hand

we've found each other again just in time
to watch the world cascading into the new age
            and coming to another end,

but this time we won't be shattered,
            we won't be parted;
                        this time we'll pass

the Guardian at the Threshold

with wounds intact
            and wake up

in the oldest of new worlds.

The Tower

The recurring dream of Babel: the monolith,
the scattering. The attempt to erect a fortress
to reach as high as the moon at whose orbit,
according to Aristotle, the kingdom of heaven
begins, a feat wholly possible if humanity
acquires the key: the universal alphabet,
and discovers how to spell magic. Then,
as the gods well know, shall we realize all
that we can imagine. Athanasius Kircher
envisioned a citadel honed like an auger
boring into the firmament, a double-helix
of criss-crossed stairs, twisting, like DNA,
that other divine ladder of language, the Logos
that encompasses beginning and end:
            everything we understand
            we learned from its ruins.

Acknowledgements

"Scintilla" and "A Spider's Worth" were previously published in *Juniper*.

"Triskelion" was previously published in *Pinhole Poetry*.

"Cat's Eye" was previously published in *The Malahat Review*, and was featured on the website Poetry Daily.

"Boreal Book of the Dead" was previously published in *High Art: Poetry Walk in High Park* (chapbook), Gesture Press, 2016.

"The Haunting, 1963" was previously published in I *Found it at the Movies*, (ed. Ruth Roach Pierson) Guernica Editions, Fall 2014.

I am grateful to editor Michael Mirolla, and to Connie McParland and Anna van Valkenburg at Guernica Editions for all the work they do. Thanks also to Errol F. Richardson for his stunning cover design.

I want to thank David Cornel and Nathan Lee, and Doug and Nancy Roorda for their love and support. Thanks also to Sue Chenette, Maureen Scott Harris, Robin Blackburn McBride, Michele Milan, Ruth Roach Pierson, Patty Rivera, Norma Rowen, Elaine Whittaker and Elana Wolff.

Completion of this book was supported by a grant from the Canada Council for the Arts, for which I am grateful.

About The Author

Julie Roorda is the author of three previous volumes of poetry, two novels, and two collections of short stories, most recently *How to Tell if Your Frog is Dead.* She lives in St. Catharines, Ontario.

Printed by Imprimerie Gauvin
Gatineau, Québec